TONGUES

Language of the Supernatural

JANET BRAZEE

All scriptures are quoted from The New King James Bible unless other-wise indicated.

Scripture quotations are taken from The New King James Version. Copyright © 1982 by Thomas Nelson, Inc. Used by permission. All rights reserved.

Scripture quotations marked (AMP) are taken from the Amplified® Bible, Copyright © 1954, 1958, 1962, 1964, 1965, 1987 by The Lockman Foundation. Used by permission. (www.Lockman.org)

ISBN: 978-0-9891429-1-5

Published by Mountz Media & Publishing
Tulsa, Oklahoma
918-296-0995
www.mountzmedia.com

Contents

CHAPTER 1

A Gift for You

Jesus had something important to say to His disciples and to you and me before He left this earth and returned to heaven. Jesus instructed Christians then and now about the infilling of the Holy Spirit and why this baptism is something we cannot do without.

Jesus gathered His followers together and shocked them. He told them it was to their advantage that He go away so He could send the Holy Spirit to them (John 16:7). He told them to wait because a promise was coming that would change their lives:

Luke 24:49 [AMP]

And behold, I will send forth upon you what My Father has promised; but remain in the city [Jerusalem] until you are clothed with power from on high.

Then before Jesus ascended to heaven, He said:

Acts 1:5,8

5 "…John truly baptized with water, but you shall be baptized with the Holy Spirit not many days from now.

8 But you shall receive power when the Holy Spirit has come upon you; and you shall be witnesses to Me in Jerusalem, and in all Judea and Samaria, and to the end of the earth."

Jesus' instructions are plain and simple: The Holy Spirit infilling is for you.

In fact, after gloriously receiving the Holy Ghost infilling on the Day of Pentecost, Peter preached to a crowd of 3,000 and even mentioned you.

Acts 2:38-39

38 Then Peter said to them, "Repent, and let every one of you be baptized in the name of Jesus Christ for the remission of sins; and you shall receive the gift of the Holy Spirit.

39 For the promise is to you and to your children, and to all who are afar off, as many as the Lord our God will call."

This verse is speaking to *you*. The promise is to *you*. You might have been afar off, but God is calling *you*. He wants *you* baptized with the Holy Ghost. It's not just for a few; it's for *you*. It's God's will that all Christians be filled with the Holy Spirit.

Some folks believe that the infilling of the Holy Spirit was only for the early Christians we read about in the book of Acts. They believe it's not for us today because tongues have passed away. But that's not what my Bible says. We just read in Acts 2:39 that "…the promise is to you and to your children, and to all who are afar off…." We qualify as "all who are afar off." We're all in that line somewhere down the road. The promise does not stop with us; it continues to our children and all who come after us.

Maybe you desire to receive the baptism of the Holy Spirit, or maybe you recently received. Maybe you received years ago, but you haven't felt free to pray in your prayer language since then. No matter which category you are in, Jesus gave you instructions.

The baptism of the Holy Ghost was never meant to be an optional experience or a one-time experience. It was not meant only for the Day of Pentecost or only for the apostles. It was not meant only for super spiritual people. It was not meant to be something we only do in church on Sundays. The baptism of the Holy Ghost is for every day of your life.

It's for yesterday, today and tomorrow.

It's a free gift available to you.

Unwrapping Your Gift

The number one reason people don't walk in the power of the Holy Ghost or take advantage of what belongs to them is a lack of knowledge. The Word of God says, "My people are destroyed for a lack of knowledge" (Hosea 4:6). Sometimes people have no idea what's available to them just like when Paul preached to the believers in Ephesus. When he asked them about the Holy Ghost, their response was, "We have not so much as heard whether there is a Holy Spirit" (Acts 19:2).

There are still believers today who have no idea there is such a thing as praying in tongues because they also lack knowledge. Yet the baptism of the Holy Ghost belongs to every born-again Christian. Notice what Jesus Himself told His disciples:

John 14:16-17 [AMP]

And I will ask the Father, and He will give you another Comforter (Counselor, Helper, Intercessor, Advocate, Strengthener, and Standby), that He may remain with you forever—The Spirit of Truth, Whom the world cannot receive (welcome, take to its heart), because it does not see Him or know and recognize Him. But you know and recognize Him, for He lives with you [constantly] and will be in you.

John the Baptist also spoke of this baptism to come in Matthew 3 when Jesus came to the River Jordan to be baptized in water:

Matthew 3:11

I indeed baptize you with water unto repentance, but He who is coming after me is mightier than I, whose sandals I am not worthy to carry. He will baptize you with the Holy Spirit and fire.

Jesus gave the Great Commission to the Church before He left this earth and specifically mentioned our supernatural language in verse 17 below:

Mark 16:15-18

15 And He said to them, "Go into all the world and preach the gospel to every creature.

16 He who believes and is baptized will be saved; but he who does not believe will be condemned.

17 And these signs will follow those who believe: In My name they will cast out demons; they will speak with new tongues;

18 they will take up serpents; and if they drink anything deadly, it will by no means hurt them; they will lay hands on the sick, and they will recover."

Speaking with new tongues is one of the signs that should follow we who believe.

That's why I thank God for the Charismatic Move of the 1960s and 1970s when the baptism of the Holy Spirit jumped over denominational barriers. Catholics, Baptists, Methodists, Presbyterians, Lutherans and those of every other denomination were gloriously filled with the Holy Ghost. It's for anyone and everyone who believes. The only thing that can stop you and me from receiving this free gift is a lack of knowledge.

A lot of times people are held back from receiving the infilling or baptism of the Holy Ghost because they have preconceived ideas of what it's like to receive. Primarily, many people think it's difficult to receive this gift. But God wouldn't offer a free gift and then make it difficult to receive. That wouldn't make sense.

If God has a gift for us, then God wants us to have it. Nothing God has for us is difficult to receive. Receiving salvation is not difficult. All we have to do is believe in our hearts and confess with our mouths that Jesus is Lord (Romans 10:9-10). The same way we receive the gift of salvation is the same way we receive every other gift God has for us.

Receiving by Faith

"But *how* do we actually receive a gift from God?" someone asks. The answer is simple. We receive by faith. "Where do we get faith?" The Bible tells us faith comes by hearing and hearing God's Word (Romans 10:17). As we hear God's Word, faith rises in our spirits or hearts. If we hear God's Word on salvation, faith comes to receive salvation. If we hear God's Word on the baptism of the Holy Ghost, faith comes to receive this wonderful infilling. As long as we hear God's Word, we cannot stop faith from coming because the Word delivers it to us.

This point was really driven home to me when my husband, Mark, was teaching our World Outreach Church congregation a series for several weeks on the importance of praying in other tongues. My faith level soared. I found myself praying in other tongues almost around the clock. I prayed in the Holy Ghost while I was getting dressed, putting on makeup and driving in traffic. I woke up early in the morning praying in tongues and fell asleep late at night praying in tongues.

Why? It happened because I was full of God's Word on the topic. I heard and kept hearing God's Word about the Holy Spirit infilling, and faith rose up in me. It's no different for you. You're hearing God's Word right now about the importance of praying in other tongues, and faith is rising in your heart. The Word is working in you, inspiring you to pray more often, giving you a desire to pray with more freedom or giving you faith to receive for the first time.

No Wailing Needed

I remember years ago we were invited to travel with a ministry team to Honduras for an outdoor evangelistic crusade. The minister on stage had given an altar call for people to come forward to receive the Holy Spirit. Hundreds of people hurried out of the bleachers down to the center of the stadium and crowded around the platform waiting to receive.

Mark and I were standing off to the side watching when suddenly, the minister ran off the platform. We found out later he was attacked with a case of "Montezuma's Revenge." Let's just say it's not a pleasant thing that sometimes hits folks traveling to foreign countries, and when it hits, a person better run for his or her life to the nearest restroom.

In the meantime, the hundreds of people standing at the base of the platform were pleading, "Oh, God, please fill me with the Holy Spirit! Oh God! Please! Please! Fill me!" There was mass wailing. Mark and I were on the edge of the platform looking at an empty stage. No minister was present. No one was in control of the service, and hundreds of people were crying, begging and wailing at the top of their lungs.

Mark looked at me and said, "Get up there and do something!"

"Excuse me?!" I said. I was thinking, *I'm just a little wife along for the ride.*

"Get up there and do something *now!*" he said. Mark knew very well that through the years I had assisted in prayer rooms all across the country when I traveled with a singing group on the late Rev. Kenneth E. Hagin's crusade team, and I had run the prayer rooms in our own ministry for years and years. I had plenty of experience getting people saved and filled. I just had never before been faced with hundreds of wailing people who were expecting another minister altogether.

So I started toward the platform thinking, *These people will have no idea who I am*. When I reached the microphone I said, "Hello. Excuse me! Excuse me!"

No reaction. They couldn't hear me past their wailing.

"Stop!" I finally screamed in the microphone.

Immediately they stopped and looked at me with daggers like, *How dare you interrupt our praying!*

Yet, their wailing wasn't praying at all. Wailing and begging are not how we receive from God. It's not necessary, and it's not godly.

I explained, "Hundreds of you came forward because you want to receive the Holy Ghost, and God wants you filled today. It's a free gift for you. So let me instruct you for a few minutes from the Word of God on how to receive. Then we will pray a mass prayer, and you will receive."

They just stared at me. I shared with them many of the scriptures from God's Word we have looked at and will look at in the next few chapters. And do you know what? In a matter of 10 minutes, we prayed a mass prayer, and they all began praying in the Holy Ghost. There were too many people to lay hands on them, but a roar of Holy Ghost supernatural language of tongues flooded heaven. All they had to hear was what the Word of God said concerning how to receive, and they instantly received.

I am a 100% believer that if we take the time to understand the Bible pattern to receive the baptism of the Holy Spirit, it's as easy as praying the prayer of salvation.

As a child I remember going to church camp where leaders prayed with me to receive the infilling of the Spirit. I still remember people on either side of me yelling instructions. One person yelled, "Let go! Let go! Just let go!" A person on the other side yelled, "Hold on! Hold on! Just hold on!" I remember thinking, *What am I supposed to let go of? How am I supposed to hold on?* Obviously, I didn't receive at that point.

Later on when I was eight years old, I received simply and easily all by myself in a church my daddy pastored. I still remember the moment. At the end of a service, I was standing by the end of an aisle, and I just began praying in other tongues. I didn't need anybody to yell in my ear. I didn't need anybody to scream at me. The Holy Ghost simply filled me to overflowing, and I received a supernatural language of tongues.

The people in Honduras received, and I received because faith comes by hearing and hearing the Word of God. As we take hold of the truths of God's Word, they will help us walk in what belongs to us.

Who Qualifies to Receive

As we read earlier, Paul asked the believers in Ephesus, "Have ye received the Holy Ghost *since ye believed?*"(Acts 19:2 KJV). In other words, if you're a believer, you're ready to receive. That's the only requirement to receive the baptism of the Holy Ghost. Receiving is not based on works. It's not based on what you have done or have not done. It's not based on how long you've been born again. If you're saved, you're ready.

Jesus Himself said if you desire to receive the Holy Ghost baptism all you have to do is ask. It doesn't get much simpler than that.

Luke 11:9-13

9 "So I say to you, ask, and it will be given to you; seek, and you will find; knock, and it will be opened to you.

10 For everyone who asks receives, and he who seeks finds, and to him who knocks it will be opened.

11 If a son asks for bread from any father among you, will he give him a stone? Or

if he asks for a fish, will he give him a ser-
pent instead of a fish?

12 Or if he asks for an egg, will he offer
him a scorpion?

13 If you then, being evil, know how
to give good gifts to your children,
how much more will your heavenly
Father give the Holy Spirit to those
who ask Him!"

All Means All

On the Day of Pentecost, 120 asked for
the Holy Ghost and received the Holy Ghost.
They waited in the Upper Room, and they
were not disappointed.

Acts 2:1-3

1 When the Day of Pentecost had fully
come, they were all with one accord in
one place.

2 And suddenly there came a sound from heaven, as of a rushing mighty wind, and it filled the whole house where they were sitting.

3 Then there appeared to them divided tongues, as of fire, and one sat upon each of them.

4 And they were all filled with the Holy Spirit and began to speak with other tongues, as the Spirit gave them utterance.

How many were filled? 10%? 50%? 99%? No. God's Word doesn't say a portion of them were filled. It says "…they were *all* filled…." How many is *all*? All. All is every last one of them.

What does that mean to you and me? It means that it is God's will that you be filled. If you've heard teaching to the contrary, forget it. You just read from God's Word that it is God's will that you be filled, and faith begins where the will of God is known. You cannot have faith to be filled with the Holy Ghost if you're not sure it's God's will.

We don't read about a select or special group who received in the Upper Room. No, Acts 2 was a pattern to show us that all who seek the Holy Ghost find the Holy Ghost. Acts 2 was the initial outpouring of the baptism of the Holy Ghost. Yet, time and time again throughout the book of Acts, we see where the Holy Ghost was poured out and people spoke with tongues.

Let's look at several examples.

About eight years after the Day of Pentecost, Philip preached a crusade in Samaria where the entire city got saved. Then Peter and John followed up getting the people filled with the Holy Ghost.

Acts 8:5,14-17

5 Then Philip went down to the city of Samaria and preached Christ to them.

14 Now when the apostles who were at Jerusalem heard that Samaria had received the word of God, they sent Peter and John to them,

15 who, when they had come down, prayed for them that they might receive the Holy Spirit.

16 For as yet He had fallen upon none of them. They had only been baptized in the name of the Lord Jesus.

17 Then they laid hands on them, and they received the Holy Spirit.

Simon was intrigued when he saw the results of Peter and John laying hands on the people. In fact, he tried to buy the gift of the Holy Spirit (Acts 8:18-25). Simon thought, *Can I give you money, and do what you do?* Obviously Simon saw something happening when hands were laid on these people. He saw an outward manifestation of an inward Holy Ghost baptism.

About 10 years after the Day of Pentecost, Peter preached to the Gentiles who got saved and filled with the Spirit:

Acts 10:44-46

44 While Peter was still speaking these words, the Holy Spirit fell upon all those who heard the word.

45 And those of the circumcision who believed were astonished, as many as came with Peter, because the gift of the Holy Spirit had been poured out on the Gentiles also.

46 For they heard them speak with tongues and magnify God.

About 20 years after the Day of Pentecost, Paul prayed with believers at Ephesus:

Acts 19:1-2,6

1 And it happened, while Apollos was at Corinth, that Paul, having passed through the upper regions, came to Ephesus. And finding some disciples

2 he said to them, "Did you receive the Holy Spirit when you believed?" So they said to him, "We have not so much as heard whether there is a Holy Spirit."

6 And when Paul had laid hands on them, the Holy Spirit came upon them, and they spoke with tongues and prophesied.

Initial Evidence

Throughout these scriptures, we've seen that every time believers are filled with the Holy Ghost, there is always an immediate initial evidence. This initial sign does not happen six months or six years down the road. When we are filled with the Holy Ghost, immediately we speak in other tongues.

"Wait a minute," somebody says. "My case is different." No, it isn't. The Bible tells us exactly how we receive. The truth is, we cannot go by our experiences—yours or mine. We must go by what the Word of God says. If our experiences line up with God's Word, hallelujah! Praise the Lord! If our experiences don't line up with God's Word, then we need to disregard them.

The Bible is very specific about this. It says, "They were all filled with the Holy Spirit and began to speak with other tongues…." (Acts 2:4). When did they speak? When they were filled. And if they did, we will.

Get Filled and Stay Filled

"But I received one time a long time ago, and that was the end of it." That's not the way God wants it to be. The Bible tells us that being filled with the Holy Ghost is *not* a one-time experience. It's power for living life. Don't leave home without it!

Praying in tongues one time is not the end of your Holy Ghost infilling; it's only the beginning. Notice what Ephesians 5 tells us:

Ephesians 5:18

Do not be drunk with wine, in which is dissipation; but be filled with the Spirit,

The word *filled* in the Greek language means literally *be being filled*. In other words, to be filled with the Holy Ghost is the continual act of being filled. Praying in tongues once is not even remotely all there is. We need to get filled and stay filled with the Holy Ghost. It's power that will carry us through life.

CHAPTER 2

Benefits of Praying in Tongues

God built into every human being a desire for the supernatural, and the baptism of the Holy Ghost is a gateway into the supernatural realm and more of God in our lives. In fact, the baptism of the Holy Ghost will make a huge difference in our Christian walk. Sometimes people wonder, *What is the big deal about speaking in tongues? Why is it so important?* Truth be told, there are so many benefits of praying in tongues it would be hard to list them all, but let's focus on a few especially important ones.

Divine Secrets

When we pray in other tongues, we don't have a clue what we're saying. Yet, the Bible tells us that God understands every word. It's almost like a heavenly Morse code. Even the devil cannot understand what's being said when we pray in tongues. It's a supernatural, spiritual language imparted to us by the Holy Ghost.

Notice what 1 Corinthians 14 tells us.

1 Corinthians 14:2

For he who speaks in a tongue does not speak to men but to God, for no one un-

derstands him; however, in the spirit he
speaks mysteries.

The Amplified Bible says we speak "se-
cret truths." I like that. When we pray in
our supernatural language, we are sharing
secrets with God. We're exchanging divine
secrets as we commune with God Almighty.

Think about the advantage this gives
us. You're not limited to your knowledge or
earthly knowledge. You're not limited to your
vocabulary. You're not limited by how well
you express yourself.

We only know so much in any situation,
so we can only pray so far on our own. Yet,
the Spirit of God who lives on the inside of us
is limited by nothing. He knows everything
about everything. So when we pray in other tongues, we hook up with the Holy Ghost

who knows all things. That means there's no telling what we pray about when we pray in other tongues, but God knows.

You might be praying for a missionary in Zimbabwe. You might be praying for someone in Antarctica. You might be praying for your children, their futures, their careers, their spouses. You might be praying for your spouse or your spouse yet to come. You might be praying for yourself. You might be praying for protection for yourself or someone else. You might be praying about a matter of life and death. You just never know. You may never know. And it doesn't matter because God knows, and He uses the supernatural prayer language flowing through you to pray about things that need prayer.

Charges You Up

Praying in tongues edifies or builds up your spirit. Look with me at 1 Corinthians 14.

1 Corinthians 14:4

He who speaks in a tongue edifies himself....

Paul is telling us that when we pray in tongues, we edify or build up our spirit in the same way a body builder lifts weights to build his or her strength. When we pray in tongues, we exercise the hidden man of the heart (1 Peter 3:4).

"But I prayed in tongues, and I didn't feel anything," someone might say. We're not talking about what you feel; we're talking about what you believe *by faith*. The Bible says that the just shall live by faith (Hebrews

37

10:38). Sure, we have feelings, but we're not supposed to live by them. We walk by faith and not by feelings.

The book of Jude tells us something important on this topic.

Jude 20

But you, beloved, building yourselves up on your most holy faith, praying in the Holy Spirit.

Again, the Bible likens praying in the Holy Ghost to building yourself up because when you pray in tongues, you build the inward man not the outward man. You build yourself up spiritually.

Actually, praying in tongues is like charging a cell phone or laptop computer. When a battery dies, we plug in to the power. Think about it. We take a cord and plug one end into the equipment with the dead battery, and we plug the other end into an electrical outlet. When the wire connects to the power source, bam! The item charges and is once again full of power.

Praying in the Holy Ghost is your power source. It's your connection to heaven. All the power in heaven is transmitted to you when you pray in the Holy Ghost. It charges up your inner man. It makes you strong. It gets you going. It's power where you need power.

When discouragement tries to harass you with thoughts of "Poor ole me!" rise up and throw it off because you're charged up with the Holy Ghost. Instead of yielding to discouragement or anything else the devil tries to bring your way, you can rise up strong because you've been charging up your inner man praying in the Holy Ghost.

More Conscious of God

The apostle Paul tells us something amazing in 1 Corinthians:

1 Corinthians 3:16

Do you not know that you are the temple of God and that the Spirit of God dwells in you?

What's just as amazing is how real this truth becomes as we pray in tongues. Praying in tongues causes us to become more and more aware of God Almighty living in us to the point that we become God-inside minded. We should begin every day with this reality and then look at ourselves in the mirror and say, *Where I go, God goes. What I say, God says. What I do, God does.* Living this way will change everything about us and around us.

Sensitize Your Spirit

Every time we pray in tongues, we sensitize and fine-tune our spirits. We develop our spirits to dominate our minds and bodies. We process the plan of God for our lives. And it becomes easier to recognize God's direction in our lives.

"But I haven't got an hour to pray in tongues every day," somebody says. Have you got 15 minutes? Have you got five minutes here and there? Don't miss out because you can't find a whole hour to pray every day. Pray in the time you do have. Pray in the shower. Pray on the way to school. Pray on the way to work. Just pray in tongues!

"What if I don't feel any different?" someone asks. Praying in tongues is not a feeling. Feelings might eventually show up, but they don't change anything. You might pray in other tongues for 30 minutes and not feel a thing; that doesn't mean nothing was accomplished. What it means is that you exercised your inward man; you energized and sensitized your spirit.

As we pray in tongues, we're spending time with the Holy Ghost, and it becomes easier and easier for us to recognize His leading and His voice. There's no short cut in getting to know a person. We must spend time with them. For example, because I know my husband's voice well, I can pick out his voice anytime anywhere.

Let's say Mark was in a room talking with many other people. Even if I walked blindfolded into the room, I would still find him. I might stumble over a few chairs, but I would eventually make my way to Mark because I know his voice. I've spent so much time with him that I could pick out his voice over every other because I *recognize* his voice.

It's the same with the Holy Ghost. The more you pray in the Holy Ghost, the more sensitive you become to His voice. This is important because life is full of choices. If we're sensitive to His voice, He can help us make the right choices.

"What does that have to do with praying in tongues?" somebody might ask. A lot. The Holy Ghost lives inside us, so He guides from inside us. If we pray in tongues often and sensitize our spirits to His voice, it will make it a whole lot easier for us to hear from Him. He is always leading us—no exceptions. Romans 8:14 says, "For as many as are led by the Spirit of God, these are sons of God." There's no question about Him leading. The whole point is that we need to be sensitive enough to follow. (Pastor Mark Brazee teaches more on this topic in his book titled *The Guide Inside*.)

As I look back over my life, it's just amazing how God got me to the right place at the right time. When I made important decisions that affected my future, most of the time I didn't realize until afterward how important certain decisions were. It's probably the same with you. That's why we need to pray more and pray often in the Holy Ghost. The more we pray in tongues, the more sensitive we become to His voice and to His leading.

Help in Prayer

The Holy Ghost is a big help in our prayer lives. The apostle Paul explains how in Romans 8.

Romans 8:26-27

26 Likewise the Spirit also helps in our weaknesses. For we do not know what we should pray for as we ought, but the Spirit Himself makes intercession for us with groanings which cannot be uttered.

27 Now He who searches the hearts knows what the mind of the Spirit is, because He makes intercession for the saints according to the will of God.

I'm sure you have found yourself in a situation where you need to pray but didn't know how to pray. I have. You might sense in your spirit that a person or situation needs prayer, but you don't know the details or God's will in the matter. That's when praying in the Holy Ghost comes in handy because you can pray divine mysteries, and God understands every word. More importantly, you can be confident you're praying in line with God's will. You may not know God's will, but the Holy Ghost does. Praying in your supernatural language comes directly out of your spirit and bypasses your mind altogether.

So when you pray in tongues, there's no room for your opinions, ideas or desires to get in the middle and mess things up. When situations come across your heart and mind, say to the Holy Ghost, "You know all things. You know the ins and outs of this situation, so I'll be a vessel. Pray through me." He's the One with the plan.

Stimulates Your Faith

Praying in tongues will stimulate our faith. As we mentioned earlier, faith only comes one way—by hearing and hearing the Word of God (Romans 10:17). But praying in tongues will help us act on the faith we do have. Sometimes we lack confidence in our faith, but praying in other tongues stimulates us to step out.

Pray in the Holy Ghost if you find your-self up against a situation where you think, *I don't know if I have the faith to believe God.* Your faith will be stirred. As Jude 20 says, "...building yourselves up on your most holy faith, praying in the Holy Spirit."

When we're in the middle of a faith challenge, it's important we don't get weary in well-doing (Galatians 6:9). If the Bible tells us not to get weary in well-doing, then I'm convinced opportunities to get weary will present themselves. What should we do when they come? Pray in the Holy Spirit to build ourselves up. Our supernatural language gives us the extra oomph needed in whatever situation we find ourselves.

A Refreshing

As the prophet Isaiah looked ahead to the promise of the Holy Spirit infilling, he told us that praying in tongues would be a rest and a refreshing. Notice his words below:

Isaiah 28:11-12

11 For with stammering lips and another tongue He will speak to this people,

12 To whom He said, "This *is* the rest *with* which You may cause the weary to rest," And, "This *is* the refreshing"; Yet they would not hear.

Then look at a New Testament scripture in Acts 3 that speaks of refreshing.

Acts 3:19

Repent therefore and be converted, that your sins may be blotted out, so *that times of refreshing may come from the presence of the Lord.*

When we pray in the Holy Ghost, we're rested and refreshed in the presence of God. We commune with God and share divine secrets and mysteries. As we continue spending time with Him, we become saturated in His presence. Sometimes people go on vacations only to return home so tired they need another vacation. But when we're refreshed by the presence of God, we're refreshed from the inside out. Nothing refreshes us like His presence.

Giving Thanks

Praying in tongues helps you give thanks to God. It will help you praise and worship. In fact, notice what Paul says in 1 Corinthians 14.

1 Corinthians 14:15 (KJV)

What is it then? I will pray with the spirit, and I will pray with the understanding also: I will sing with the spirit, and I will sing with the understanding also.

Paul is explaining that we will pray in our known language and then switch over to our supernatural language. He goes on to say that we will sing in our known language and then switch over and sing in our supernatural language.

Often when we praise and worship God, we run out of words to express how great God is and how much we love Him. But when we begin communicating with Him through our supernatural language, we no longer are limited. Our hearts are free.

Ephesians 5 tells us how we can worship supernaturally.

Ephesians 5:18-20

18 And do not be drunk with wine, in which is dissipation; but be filled with the Spirit,

19 speaking to one another in psalms and hymns and spiritual songs, singing and making melody in your heart to the Lord,

20 giving thanks always for all things to God the Father in the name of our Lord Jesus Christ.

Full of the Holy Ghost, we can hook our mouths to our spirits and not only pray, but also speak to one another in "psalms and hymns and spiritual songs, singing and making melody in our hearts." What a help this supernatural language is to live the supernatural life God intended us to live.

Train the Human Tongue

Praying in tongues trains the human tongue, and we all know our tongues need to be trained and controlled. Instead of saying something unkind and having to repent later, we ought to pray in tongues. It accomplishes a lot more. When I'm not happy with someone, I pray in tongues for the person. It's the only thing that will bring change to the situation, and it trains my tongue at the same time.

James 3:5 says, "Even so the tongue is a little member and boasts great things. See how great a forest a little fire kindles!" In other words, your tongue can cause quite a stir. The best thing you can do for an unruly tongue is to control it by praying in your supernatural language. Here's my motto: Bite your tongue and pray in tongues. It can save you—and other people—lots of tears.

Once words are spoken, they're out there, and there's no taking them back. The little phrase, "Sticks and stones may break my bones, but words can never hurt me" is not true. Words are powerful. They have the power to create, but they also have the power to destroy. Watch your words. When you're tempted to fly off the handle, pull yourself away from the situation and pray in tongues.

Keep Yourself in the Love of God

Praying in tongues will increase our ability to walk in love and keep us in the love of

God. As long as we're on this earth, there will be opportunities to become offended and opportunities to choose whether or not we walk in love. Actually, we pretty much make that choice on a daily basis. Usually the folks who challenge us the most are those closest to us because the devil knows they can hurt us the most.

I remember many years ago when Mark and I had been ministering in Europe, some friends wanted to meet with us the night before we left. They felt we should know some things being said about us. We were shocked. The comments being spread about us were not true at all, and the people saying them were close to us and knew better. I was deeply upset.

When Mark and I got back to our hotel, I couldn't sleep. I was so bothered by it all that I tossed and turned all night. Even while we were packing and traveling to the airport the next morning, I said very little. I was so hurt I couldn't talk. Thoughts bombarded my mind, and all I could do was try to figure out why these people would say such things.

A few minutes after the plane took off, I was still sitting quietly with tears running down my cheeks. I finally thought, *I will just close my eyes and sleep, hoping it all goes away. At least I won't have to think anymore for a while.*

The minute I closed my eyes, I heard down on the inside loudly and clearly, "Keep yourself in the love of God, praying in the Holy Ghost." It wasn't an audible voice, but it might as well have been. The Spirit of God made Himself loud and clear. So I began to pray in tongues under my breath until I drifted off to sleep. When I woke up, all the hurt was gone. All the sadness was gone. All the questions were gone. It was totally supernatural.

I looked over at Mark and told him what happened. "That's amazing," he said. "Just before you fell asleep, I almost leaned over and said, 'Why don't you pray in tongues for a while.'"

"It's a good thing you didn't!" I said. "That was not what I wanted to hear at that moment."

"I kind of figured that," he smiled and said.

The Holy Ghost knew I needed to hear it anyway, and He told me. Right away I looked up the verse the Holy Ghost had quoted. Keep in mind that Bible translators divided the Bible into chapters and verses, but really the verses in Jude 20 and 21 are all one thought. Let's look at it again:

Jude 20-21

20 But you, beloved, building yourselves up on your most holy faith, *praying in the Holy Spirit,*

21 *keep yourselves in the love of God,* looking for the mercy of our Lord Jesus Christ unto eternal life.

I had never before connected the two thoughts until the Holy Ghost spoke to me that day. He gave me good advice. From personal experience, I can tell you that praying in tongues can help us walk in love in the toughest situations. I'm a living witness.

Let's face facts. People will hurt and disappoint us. Yet, the best way to handle whatever comes along is to pray in tongues, keeping ourselves in the love of God. Walking in love is a serious thing because faith works by love, and the just are to live by faith. So faith and love must be our way of life.

I could have chosen to get offended and stay offended, but that only would have hurt me. The other folks would have gone their merry ways without even knowing I was offended. The truth is, walking in love is easier said than done. Yet, God expects us to choose the high road, and praying in tongues is one way we do it.

Quiet Your Busy Mind

Praying in the Holy Ghost will help turn off your busy mind and keep you focused on God's Word. The Bible says there are many voices in this world, but the only voice that counts is God's. When we pray in the Holy Ghost, we pray from our spirits so the fiery darts and worries attacking our minds are stopped.

When you pray in tongues, your mind will get quiet to hear what your mouth is saying. And since your mind won't understand one word of your supernatural language, it will eventually just get quiet.

As we pray, our minds may be thinking, *This does not make sense! This will never work! I'm going to fail! How can God help me this time?* But our spirits can be at rest in the

Word and the Spirit. God leads us on the inside with a velvety knowing, a peace that passes all understanding. And peace is what we must follow. The Bible says we are to be led forth with peace. Peace is what guides us and keeps us. So pray in your supernatural language until peace saturates you from head to toe.

Help Through Hard Times

Praying in tongues will help us get through hard times. "What hard times?" someone might ask. I hate to break it to you, but the Bible never promised that Christians would be redeemed from hard times. In fact, hard times come to everyone. Thank God, we do not have to be caught off guard, and we don't have to handle trouble like the world does.

We've got the answer. We've got the victory. We've got the Word. We've got the Holy Ghost. And as we plug in to God's Word and pray in our supernatural language, strength and insight come to handle the hard times.

James gives us good advice:

James 5:13-15 (KJV)

13 Is any among you afflicted? let him pray. Is any merry? let him sing psalms.

14 Is any sick among you? let him call for the elders of the church; and let them pray over him, anointing him with oil in the name of the Lord:

15 And the prayer of faith shall save the sick, and the Lord shall raise him up....

For years I read this scripture, assuming I knew what it meant. I was sure the word *afflicted* meant *sick*. But that's not what it means at all. Actually, theses verses even give different instructions to those who are afflicted and those who are sick, so obviously *afflicted* and *sick* don't mean the same thing. The sick person is told to call for the elders of the church so they can pray and anoint the sick person with oil in the name of the Lord.

Those who are afflicted are told to do something for themselves. In fact, according to The New Strong's Exhaustive Concordance of the Bible, the word *afflicted* in the original Greek means to *undergo hardship, suffer trouble.* In other words, the afflicted person is facing temptation, test or trial and just plain having a hard time. That puts a whole different spin on things. What is the afflicted person supposed to do? Pray! This verse basically says, "Hey, anyone out there having a hard time? Anyone out there in trouble and need help? If you feel like you're hitting your head against a wall and not getting anywhere in a bad situation, here's what you should do: *Pray!*"

Don't have a pity party and call your friends to join you. Instead, James says to get busy praying. You can pray in your known language if you want, but at a certain point, you'll run out of knowledge and words.

That's when you should switch over and let the Holy Ghost help you pray.

The Holy Ghost has all the answers. If you need help, the Holy Ghost will help you. He's your Helper, and He will sure help you pray. Your faith will be stirred. Your spirit will be stimulated. Your hard time will turn around.

So often growing up, my daddy would conclude services in the church he pastored by opening the altars for prayer. He would say, "If you need to pray through, come up around the altar." Actually, we don't hear the expression *pray through* much these days. But the truth is, often times we need to pray through. "Pray through what?" someone might ask. Pray through the hard times.

When hard times stare you in the face, don't stay there. Pray your way out!

Poke a hole in that hard time with your supernatural language and break through to victory.

Don't let hard times put you under. Come out on top. You cannot do it in your own strength, but you can do it through God and His Word. I don't care how long you've been born again. You need the help of the Holy One. He said, if you're afflicted and having hard times, you need to pray.

Don't call the Prayer Tower; call on God. The Prayer Tower is good, but it doesn't replace your supernatural prayer language, which is better because it's direct communication between God and you. In fact, if you're afflicted, the Bible doesn't tell you to call anybody at all; the Bible tells you to pray. God has given you the victory, and it's yours for the taking. Some days you may not feel like you have the victory, but those are the days when you should double up your time in the Word and double up your time praying in tongues.

Now we understand why Jesus told the disciples not to leave Jerusalem without the Holy Ghost. Jesus didn't want His followers to miss out on the baptism of the Holy Ghost because it's an important part of living a victorious Christian life.

Do you see why the devil has fought it for so many years? If the devil can keep us blinded to the importance of praying in the Holy Ghost, the body of Christ will be weak and without power. The body won't know what to do when hard times come. It won't know how to process the plans of God through prayer. It won't know how to stimulate its faith. It will be limited by its known language instead of equipped with a supernatural language that speaks divine secrets and mysteries to God.

Power to Witness

Last but not least, we read in Acts 2 that when the Holy Ghost came rushing in the Upper Room, He came as *fire*. Yet, throughout the Old Testament when the glory of God filled the tabernacle, it came in the form of a cloud. So why was there not a cloud in the Upper Room denoting the presence of

God? Zechariah 10:1 says ask the Lord for rain, and He will send rain. So why was there not rain in the Upper Room denoting the glory of God? A cloud or rain would have been pretty spectacular.

Have you wondered why the Holy Ghost chose to come as fire? If you've ever been caught on fire, you wouldn't have to ask that question. I have.

Several years ago my husband took me out to dinner at our favorite little Italian place. The lights were dim with candles on the table, and we enjoyed a wonderfully romantic dinner. Eventually, the waiter came by asking if we wanted dessert. Mark said, "I'll take some cheesecake." "I'll just have a bite of his," I said.

Dessert came, and we were engrossed in conversation. All of the sudden, I realized, *Hmmm, Mark is devouring that cheesecake and hasn't asked me if I want a bite.* So I thought, *Every "man" for himself.* I picked up my fork and reached across the table to get my bite. When I did, the sleeve of my sweater got too close to the candle in the middle of the table.

I was on fire!

Flames were at my wrist quickly climbing up my sweater sleeve.

In the middle of that quiet, little romantic restaurant, I jumped to my feet and screamed at the top of my lungs, "JESUS! JESUS! JESUS!" My fork went flying in the air along with my bite of cheesecake. I hopped and screamed and waved my arms all at the same time. I was on fire, and the whole restaurant knew it.

With my life flashing before me, I looked down at my husband hoping he would help save me only to realize he was still seated at the table calmly eating his cheesecake. I thought I was dying and looked at him with fear in my eyes, but he looked back at me, put his finger to his mouth and said, "Shhh!" Think about that now. I was on fire, but he told me to be quiet.

It was easy for him to quietly sit in his chair. He wasn't on fire. But let me tell you, when people are on fire, they don't sit still. They're not quiet.

It's the same spiritually.

When we're not on fire spiritually, it's easy to sit in a pew Sunday after Sunday dead as a doornail. It's easy to unemotionally check our watches to see if church is about over so the pot roast in the oven at home won't burn. But when we're on fire for God, we cannot contain ourselves.

That's why the Holy Ghost showed up as fire in the Upper Room.

Jeremiah put it this way: The anointing of God is like fire shut up in our bones (Jeremiah 20:9).

When you are on fire, you don't care who knows it.

The Holy Ghost sat on those in the Upper Room with fire so they could sit no longer. They had to get up and do something for God. That's why Jesus said wait for the promise. You will be baptized in the Holy

Ghost, and the power of God will come on you to be a witness.

When the Holy Ghost fire comes on you, you will receive power to witness in Tulsa, in Oklahoma, in the United States and in the regions beyond.

CHAPTER 3

The Bible Pattern to Receive

In praying with literally thousands of people through the years in prayer rooms across America and overseas, I always ask this question: "On the Day of Pentecost when the Holy Ghost came rushing into the Upper Room, who spoke in tongues?" Nine out of 10 people answer me saying it was the Holy Ghost who did the speaking. Some people even say, "Well, the Holy Ghost, of course." But let's read Acts 2.

Acts 2:1-4

1 When the Day of Pentecost had fully come, they were all with one accord in one place.

2 And suddenly there came a sound from heaven, as of a rushing mighty wind, and it filled the whole house where they were sitting.

3 Then there appeared to them divided tongues, as of fire, and one sat upon each of them.

4 And they were all filled with the Holy Spirit and began to speak with other tongues, as the Spirit gave them utterance.

Let me ask again. Who began to speak? *The people.* You might remember from grammar lessons in school that the word *they* is an *understood subject* in verse 4. So the sentence actually says: They were all filled with the Holy Ghost, and they all began to speak with other tongues.

The Holy Ghost doesn't have vocal chords. He doesn't have a mouth. He doesn't have a tongue. He uses your voice, your mouth, your tongue.

Let me put it this way. If I asked, "What is your name?" would you stare at me blankly? If you did, I would never have the pleasure of knowing your name. In order for me to know your name, you would need to open your mouth and speak, "My name is…." You would need to open your mouth, use your vocal chords to produce sound, form words and speak.

It's no different when you receive the Holy Spirit. You have to open your mouth, use your vocal chords to produce sound, form words and speak.

"How is this possible?" someone might ask. It's possible because the Holy Ghost supernaturally gives us the ability. Look at verse 4 once again.

Acts 2:4

4 And they were all filled with the Holy Spirit and began to speak with other tongues, as the Spirit gave them utterance.

This verse tells us that the Holy Spirit gives the utterance or ability, and we give voice to it.

Here's the point: The supernatural part is not *who* is speaking but *what* is being spoken.

In John 7 Jesus said our supernatural language will flow out of us like rivers of living water. Jesus told the woman at the well in John 4 that once she drank the living water of salvation she would never thirst again. At the moment of salvation, the Spirit of God makes His home in every believer. Then when we're baptized in the Holy Ghost, we receive a greater measure of the Holy Ghost. The infilling is much more than a drink of water—it's *rivers*. It's more than enough water to quench a person's thirst—so much more that it flows out of us and spills on everyone else around.

At the same time, speaking in other tongues is not some kind of weird, out-of-body experience where a person gets caught up to the third heaven and speaks sounds he or she hears out in la-la-land somewhere. No, it's none of that. There's nothing strange or complicated about speaking in other tongues. When we ask the Lord to fill us with the Holy Ghost, He saturates our innermost beings or spirits, and we are given a capability we did not have before. A supernatural, heavenly prayer language flows out of our mouths.

One Language at a Time

Another point we need to understand about the Bible pattern to receive the Holy Spirit is that we cannot speak two languages simultaneously. If you know more than one language and you want to say hello, you must choose to speak in one language or the other. For instance, hello in English is *hello.* *Hello* in Spanish is *hola.* Yet, no matter how well you speak any two languages, you cannot speak them at the same time. It's no different in other tongues.

When we receive the Holy Ghost, we begin thanking Him. "Thank You, Lord, for filling me with the Holy Ghost. I believe I receive in Jesus' name." Then all English needs to stop. There must be a place where we stop speaking our known language *before* we can begin to speak our heavenly language.

You must give way to the supernatural utterance.

You must speak the supernatural sounds, syllables, partial syllables or words that He gives you. This is where faith comes in. You have to open up your mouth and say something that you don't understand, something that makes no sense to your mind. And as you trust the Holy Ghost to give you supernatural words, He will.

One Word at a Time

How do you begin speaking a whole language? One word at a time. It's the same way when you speak in tongues. You start with a sound or a syllable and grow from there. When a child learns how to speak, he or she doesn't wake up at 12 or 18 months, walk into the kitchen one morning and say, "Hey, Mom and Dad, what's for breakfast?" If a toddler does that, you let me know. I would want to meet the child, as would scientists and news reporters around the world.

I remember when my 18-month great niece said to my sister, Renee, on the phone, "Mi-mi!" My sister called me ecstatically. It may not thrill you, but it thrilled my sister. She didn't hear whole sentences like, "Mimi, I love you. Mimi, I want to come see you." No, all she heard was just, *Mi-mi*. That was it, but it was a start.

For most people, that seems to be the way they first receive their heavenly language—a few syllables or a few words. I have prayed with other people who experienced an amazing, overwhelming flow of language rolling out of them. Yet, more times than not, most people begin with a few sounds and words.

It's 'Just Me'

Often when people first receive their prayer language, they become discouraged thinking, *I feel like it's just me!* Yes! It *is* you. *You* are opening your mouth. *You* are producing the sound. *You* are speaking words the Holy Ghost gives you and only God understands.

Keep speaking!

The more you pray in tongues, the more words you will have. It's like the sip of water that turns into a river. Look specifically at what Jesus said in John 7:

John 7:38

He who believes in Me, as the Scripture has said, out of his heart will flow rivers of living water.

Your river may start off like a trickle, but that's all right. Keep with it. Keep yielding to the Holy Ghost, and soon, it will flow like a river.

How many adults do you know who still say *Mama* and *Dada*? Of course you don't know any. Yet, these same adults probably began with syllables something like *Ma* or *Da* that grew to *Mama* and *Dada* and eventually became *Mom* and *Dad*. As they spoke the words they had, more words came and an entire language developed. It's no different with your heavenly prayer language.

If a whole language flows out of you when you first receive the baptism of the Holy Ghost, great. Go for it! But if you only have a few words, a few syllables, a few sounds, don't get discouraged. Stick with it. Continue to speak the words you have, and before long, a new word will come to you. Then by faith speak it out. The more you pray, the more this will happen. The more you speak, the more new words you will have until you're a gushing river of supernatural language.

Praying in the Holy Ghost is a language given to you, and it's an act of your will.

The Bible tells us that we can pray in tongues or sing in tongues. We can pray with our understanding or sing with our understanding. In fact, we can—and should—switch back and forth between the two. We should pray all we know in English and then allow the Holy Spirit to lead us where we could not go on our own. We can start praying when we want and stop praying when we want because it's our personal language to speak at will.

I encourage you to pray often in your supernatural language. Pray every day. Pray while getting dressed. Pray while driving. Pray when you wake up. Pray as you fall asleep. Don't get talked out of it by the devil or yourself. I remember praying with a man years ago who came back to the prayer room in one of our meetings and got gloriously re-filled with the Holy Ghost.

Later he returned and said to me, "I received my supernatural language 40 years ago, but when I walked out of church, the devil said, 'That was just you. You made the whole thing up.' I believed him, and I never prayed in tongues again."

"But now," he said, "I understand that, of course, I'm the one doing the speaking. It's the words the Holy Ghost gives me that are the supernatural part." So don't let the devil lie to you. Don't you miss out on even one day of praying in your supernatural language. Pray and keep on praying. It's music to God's ears. He understands every word.

Receive!

If you are born again and you desire to receive the baptism of the Holy Spirit, we will pray at the end of this chapter. If you are not yet born again, let me encourage you to turn to page 93, and pray with me now. There's no better time than right now to make a fresh start in life and begin praying in your supernatural language.

Or, maybe you prayed in your supernatural language one time many years ago but felt like it was "just you." If so, yield now and more language will come. Just as sweetly and gently as the Holy Ghost came to me as I stood in my daddy's church all by myself many years ago, He will come to you now.

Let's pray. Repeat aloud:

Father, I thank You for Jesus. I thank You that He is my Lord. I also thank You for the Holy Ghost. You have given Him to me. He is a gift. I desire to be baptized in the Holy Ghost just as the people in the Upper Room were on the Day of Pentecost when they were all filled and began to speak. I ask You now to fill me with the Holy Ghost. Fill me with the power and supernatural equipping of Your Spirit that You said is so important. You said if I would ask, I would receive. So I ask You now to baptize me with the Holy Ghost.

Thank You for filling me now. By faith I will speak the syllables, sounds or words You give me. I lift my voice now and thank You in my supernatural language.

Friend, open your mouth and begin to make sounds and form words. The Holy Ghost will fill you, and you'll never be the same again.

A Fresh Start

The first step toward a fresh start and complete turnaround in your life is to receive Jesus Christ as your Lord and Savior. The minute you do, you're ready to be baptized in the Holy Spirit and begin praying in your supernatural language. This will be the best decision you've ever made. Pray this prayer aloud now.

> Dear heavenly Father:
>
> Your Word says, "Whosoever shall call on the name of the Lord shall be saved" (Acts 2:21). I call on You right now.
>
> The Bible also says if I confess with my mouth that Jesus is Lord and believe in my heart that You have raised Him from the dead, I shall be saved (Romans 10:9-10). I make that choice now.

Jesus, I believe in You. I believe in my heart and confess with my mouth that You were raised from the dead. I ask You to be my Lord and Savior. Thank You for forgiving me of all my sins. I believe I'm now a new creation in You. Old things have passed away; all things have become new in Jesus' name (2 Corinthians 5:17). Amen.

Share Your Good News

If you have received Jesus Christ as Lord or prayed in tongues for the first time, please email or call our office. We want to hear from you!

World Outreach Church
P.O. Box 470308
Tulsa, OK 74147-0308
918-461-9628
prayer@woctulsa.org

WORLD OUTREACH CHURCH

8863 E. 91st St.

Tulsa, Oklahoma

Service times — www.woctulsa.org or
918.461.9628

Live streaming and archived services —
www.woctulsa.org.

Teaching materials by Pastors Mark and
Janet Brazee and music by Pastor Janet —
www.brazee.org and the WOC Bookstore.

We're a place you can call home!